Should Kids Play Video Games?

A Persuasive Text

Written by
Tara Peterson and her fourth-grade class

MONDO

Acknowledgments

PHOTO CREDITS
Copyright © by John Paul Endress
Cover, p.1, p. 3, p. 5, p.6 (top), p. 7, p. 8, p. 10 (top), p. 11, p. 12 (top), p. 13, p. 14 (top), p. 15,
p. 16 (top), p. 18 (top), p. 20, p. 22, p. 23, p. 24, p. 25, p. 26, p. 27, p. 28

P. 8 (bottom): © Bill Aron/Photo Edit, Inc.; p. 9: © Rob Lewine/Corbis;
p. 10 (bottom): © Tony Freeman/Photo Edit, Inc.; p. 12 (bottom): Time Life Pictures/Getty Images;
p. 13: © Bonnie Kamin/Photo Edit, Inc.; p. 16 (bottom): © Jonathan Nourok/Photo Edit, Inc.;
p. 18 (bottom): Marc Romanelli/Getty Images; p. 19: © Corbis Sygma; p. 21: © Kathy Mcaughlin/The Image Works

Text copyright © 2006 by MONDO Publishing

For information contact:
MONDO Publishing
980 Avenue of the Americas
New York, NY 10018

Visit our web site at http://www.mondopub.com

Printed in the United States of America
Printed in Canada
ISBN: 1-59336-338-9

Designed by Jean Cohn

07 08 09 10 11 9 8 7 6 5 4 3 2 1

Library of Congress Cataloging-in-Publication Data
Peterson, Tara. Should kids play video games? : a persuasive text / written by Tara
Peterson with her fourth-grade class. p. cm. Summary: A fourth-grade class presents
arguments for and against playing video games. Includes bibliographical references and
index. ISBN 1-59336-338-9 (pbk.) 1. Video games--Juvenile literature. I. Title.
GV1469.3.P48 2006   794.8--dc22

Contents

Introduction

Should Kids Play Video Games?

Our class debated whether or not it is a good idea for kids to play video games. In this book we will present arguments for and against playing video games.

What Is a Video Game?

A video game is an electronic game in which images on a screen are controlled by dials and/or buttons. This can include handheld electronic games, game systems that are played on a television screen, or software for computer games. The video game has become a large part of our culture and is here to stay.

What Is a Persuasive Text?

A persuasive text is writing that tries to make the reader believe in something, one way or another. Our book is a persuasive text. We have written our opinions on the topic of playing video games and have supported our ideas with facts and examples. We read lots of magazine and newspaper articles to learn more about video games. We will try to use this information to convince you to agree with us.

Some of us believe that video games are an important part of

our lives and that kids should play them. We will argue that the games are fun, entertaining, educational, improve planning skills, and can even reduce stress.

Others in our class believe that kids should not play video games. We will tell you that video games may cause violent behavior and addiction, and that many of the games being played by children contain inappropriate material.

At the end of the book, we will show you the steps we used to write this persuasive text in case you want to write your own.

Should Kids Play Video Games? What Do You Think?

At the end of each argument, you will find either a controller or a controller with a red line through it. This is what you will see:

A controller means the argument is FOR playing video games. A controller with a red line through it means the argument is AGAINST playing video games. After reading each argument, decide how convincing you think it was and jot down a score:

3 points = strong

2 points = adequate

1 point = poor

After reading all of our arguments, add up the points you gave FOR playing video games. Then add all the points you gave AGAINST playing video games. See which side you agree with!

Video Games Are Educational

"A lot of video games are fun, educational, and entertaining—all at the same time." —ALI BOHRER AND MADISON DINASO

Many video games are fun to play and are educational, too. You might not notice how much you are learning when you play. Video games can improve math, reading, spelling, and many other skills.

For example, one computer software game allows kids to build virtual theme parks. Players have a budget to work with, and they must purchase games and rides to build their own theme park. The more rides and games they offer, the more people will come to their park, and the more money they will make. Players must make decisions and solve problems. Here is a question you might have to answer if you were playing: What do you do when someone throws a stink bomb in your theme park? The answer is to hire a custodian to clean it up. You can afford to do this if you manage your money properly. Playing this fun game can help you develop strategic planning skills.

In another educational video game, you need to answer math questions such as 6 x 4 = ? to move up to the next stage. There are different levels for players to choose from, so children of all ages can play. This teaches math skills in a fun way and provides practice for addition, subtraction, estimation, multiplication, division, fractions, decimals, and percents.

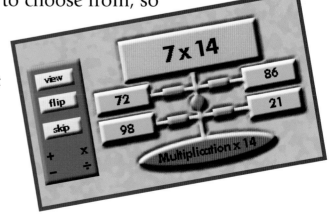

Educational software games feature sports such as basketball, soccer, hockey, football, and baseball. These video games teach kids a lot about sports because most have an information box at the corner of the screen explaining the rules of the game. Players can also learn skills such as passing a ball in basketball, by watching the player on the video game perform these skills. Kids can choose their players and compete against the computer—and learn good sportsmanship at the same time.

A lot of educational video games also feature children's favorite sports characters. Kids will have so much fun making up routines and exercises for those athletes to perform that they won't realize all the new skills they're learning!

Can you imagine a world without video games? We can't. A lot of video games are fun, educational, and entertaining— all at the same time. Why would someone object to our playing these games, especially if our homework is already done?

Video Games May be Addictive

"Playing too many video games leaves less time for more important things." —JOSH BERLOWITZ, MAIKA IKEBE, AND JULIE KIM

Beware! Video game addiction is spreading. This happens when people can't stop playing or thinking about video games. You may ask: How much time do kids spend playing video games? What can happen if people play a lot of video games? Why do they get addicted? Here are our answers to these questions.

How Much Time Do Kids Spend Playing Video Games?

Studies have shown that about 90% of households in the United States own or rent video game equipment. The average eighth-grade boy plays video games 23 hours per week, and girls play half that amount. These statistics show that many kids are spending a lot of time playing video games.

What Could Happen If You Play A Lot of Video Games?

If you play a lot of video games, you may become addicted. Playing too many video games leaves less time for more important things such as friends, family, schoolwork, homework, athletics, clubs, and sleep. If you spend less time with your friends, you may have fewer friends.

Lack of sleep can lead to poor health. Kids may come to school late or fall asleep at school if they've stayed up too late playing video games. And their grades may suffer too.

Why Do People Get Addicted?

Video games are popular and fun. That's why lots of people play video games every day. If people start playing more and more, they can become addicted. They want to learn more and more about the game and just can't stop playing. Also, they continue playing because they want to win. This constant playing can lead to addiction.

What May Happen When People Become Addicted?

People who become addicted to violent video games may become violent. There are stories in the news about kids who murdered other kids after playing these kinds of video games.

Violence is just one of many problems caused by video game addiction. Video games hurt people's lives and health by taking the place of other important activities. Now that you realize that playing too many video games can hurt you in so many ways and also be dangerous to others, don't get addicted to them!

Video Games Are Fun and Entertaining

"Video games provide hours of fun for everyone."

—LAWRENCE SLOANE AND ALEC EISENBERG

Are you a couch potato? Do you just sit on the sofa all day and watch television? If so, you are not exercising your body or mind. And it's such a waste of time! Why not play a video game instead? Such games are fun, educational, entertaining, and a great way to bring people together.

Video games are fun and entertaining. They provide hours of fun for everyone. It's not only kids who like them but adults too. In our families, our uncles, brothers, and sisters enjoy playing video games. Why should people play video games? We can give you lots of reasons.

Video games never become boring because you can always buy or rent new ones. There are now virtual-reality devices that can be hooked up to your game system.

A virtual-reality device is like a video camera that puts you into the game, and you become the controller. This means that players feel as though they're in the game.,

Video games are a fun way to spend time with your

family and friends. You and your friends can have contests—like driving and fighting. Playing video games can help bring families together too. It is really fun to play with your brothers and sisters. It can teach siblings to get along better and to enjoy spending time with each other.

If television isn't enough to keep you interested, video games will definitely get you involved. Get off that couch and go play some video games. They're entertaining and fun.

Video Games May Lead to Violence

"We believe that some video games are OK, but violent video games are terrible!" —TYLER FODIMAN AND EMILY GREENWALD

We believe that some video games are OK, but violent video games are terrible! A 2001 review of the 70 top-selling video games found that 89% of them have some kind of violence. Fifty percent have serious violence, and 40% have comic violence. Violence is the main point of 17% of these games. That's too much!

By watching and playing violent video games, the player can become aggressive and even commit murder in real life. If kids play these games too much, they may think that it is OK to kill someone, just like in the game. This is just what happens sometimes! The news has reported cases where teenagers have commited murder after playing violent video games. In one case, a 15-year-old girl and others were killed in Kentucky in a mass shooting. Another news story told about a 17-year-old boy who brutally beat and stabbed his 14-year old friend after playing a violent video game, imitating what happened in the game.

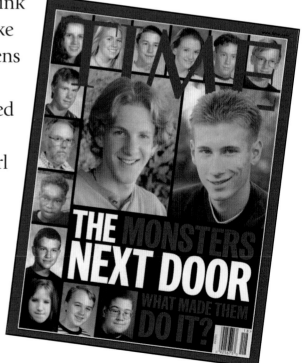

Studies have shown that video games desensitize some children to violence. When children watch violent television, they are simply viewing the violence. But when they are playing a violent video game, they are participating in the action. One child beat

up his friend so badly that it left his friend brain damaged. He told his social worker that he couldn't help himself because he felt like he was in one of his video games. When kids play violent video games, their aggressive instincts become sharpened. Some kids hurt innocent people after playing just a couple of violent video games.

In a recent survey, boys and girls from fourth to-eighth grade preferred violent video games to all other types, including general entertainment, educational, and sports games. So many children are playing violent video games, which could easily lead to more violence among children.

Companies who make violent video games are also to blame for this problem. Just because a company can make violent video games doesn't mean that it should. These companies are selling violent video games just to make money. They don't care about the kids that buy those games or if those games encourage kids to act aggressively.

Stop playing and selling violent video games before more people get hurt!

Video Games Can Help Reduce Stress

"Play a stress-reducing video game and see how relaxed you can get!"
—RACHEL WEINSTEIN AND ALEX GELB

Are you ever so mad that you want to hit someone? How about playing a video game instead? Certain video games are designed to reduce stress. The calmer you are, the easier it is to win.

How does the computer know what you are feeling? Does it read your mind? No. Sensors can be clipped to your fingers to measure your temperature and pulse rate and show how stressed out you are. What makes playing these games hard is when you are losing. You might get more stressed, which makes it harder to win. So you have to try to relax and breathe deeply if you want to win.

In one game similar to baseball, the player's stress level is measured. If you're the player and your stress level is high, you're more likely to strike out. If your stress level is low, you have a better chance at hitting a home run. The calmer you are, the more likely you are to win the game.

Some video games measure both stress level and focus. There are race car games where the goal is to travel fast enough to qualify for the next race. If the player feels too much stress and is not focusing, he or she will not do well. But if the player is calm and has good focus, the game will allow for better steering and faster speed. The player then has a good chance of qualifying for the next race.

You don't have to buy one of these particular games to reduce stress. You can turn any game into a stress-reducing game by installing a new kind of controller. The buttons become easier to use as you become more relaxed. You attach wires from the controller to your head to measure your stress level.

When you feel stressed out, now you know one thing that you can do. Play a stress-reducing video game and see how relaxed you can get!

Video Games Can't Be Properly Monitored by Parents

"Most parents don't know what video games their kids are playing." —TORI MORANO, ETHAN ADER, AND LUCAS CAHN-EVANS

Parents may not know it, but they often allow their kids to play inappropriate video games. Unless parents can be more responsible, kids should not play video games at all.

Parents should be more aware of what they are buying for their kids. Kids often ask their parents to purchase violent video games. A 1993 study by Dr. Jeanne Funk, published in a journal called *Clinical Pediatrics,* indicated that over 80% of players are playing video games with at least some violent content. Playing violent video games may cause a person to become angry. He or she may then act violently, hurting or even killing people.

Playing a violent video game is worse than watching a violent television show because the person interacts with the video game. The player gets pulled into the game and wants to repeat the action of the game. Players may become addicted and often play these games too much of the time. Spending too much

time playing violent games can lead a person to act violently even when not playing these games.

Most parents don't know what video games their kids are playing. A 1999 study found that most parents either couldn't name their kids' favorite video games or guessed incorrectly. In 70% of these wrong guesses, the child described his or her favorite game as violent.

Parents need to know what games are appropriate for their kids. They should also find out what other parents buy for their kids. Kids and parents must learn about video game ratings. Here is a brief description of the ESRB (Entertainment and Software Board) ratings system.

EC	*(Early Childhood) is for ages 3 and up.*
E	*(Everyone) has a little violence.*
E 10+	*(Everyone 10 and Older) has more violence, mild language, suggestive themes.*
T	*(Teen) has some violence and bad words, for ages 13 and up.*
M	*(Mature) has intense violence, bad language, and mature content for ages 17 and up.*
AO	*(Adults Only) has a lot of violence, mature themes, and bad language.*

Parents need to learn this ratings system. They need to pay attention to what games their kids are playing and make sure that those games are not too adult or too violent. Until parents take on this responsibility, kids should not play video games at all.

Video Games Can Teach Planning Skills

"Our parents are noticing our organizational skills improve because we play video games." —ISAMU KUBO AND TAKUYA HATTA

 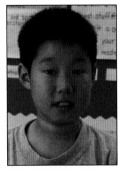

Did you ever notice that video games often teach something? Many video games can help improve a person's planning skills. In certain video games, for example, players can simulate the development of towns and cities, start businesses, and create their own movies.

Planning skills are important to have because those skills help a person think deeply to find an answer. Our parents are noticing our organizational skills improve because we play video games. These video games make us kids better at solving problems and achieving goals, skills which will be very useful when we become adults! As we focus on the games, we pick up lots of ideas on the way to do things.

In one video game, players have to pay bills and use their money to make their house or apartment comfortable. This helps children plan for their future.

Adventure video games improve children's planning skills because players have to think and plan carefully to win the game. They also teach real things that could happen in life by presenting realistic problems or having the player work in different occupations, such as the military, industry, flight training, and space exploration.

Thinking, analyzing, and planning are very important skills to have. Since some video games can help us get better at doing these things, we think kids should play video games. We hope that you agree with us!

Video Games Have a Bad Rating System

"Many video games that are rated as appropriate for young kids are actually not suitable for them."

—DANIEL WEBER, JESSICA TILLES, AND RYAN ROSENBERG

Did you know that inappropriate video games are being sold to kids? Many video games that are rated as appropriate for young kids are actually not suitable for them. Many products that are rated as not appropriate for young kids are still being sold to them. We think this is wrong, and it needs to be stopped.

A 2001 study by the Harvard School of Public Health found that the Entertainment and Software Rating Board (ESRB) often gives an E rating based on the way the video–game manufacturer describes the game. Some manufacturers don't write descriptions of their video games, so ESRB doesn't even address the violent content of those video games. This study says that 60% of the E-rated video games had violence in them, either rewarding players who injured characters or else requiring players to injure characters in order to continue playing.

We think the ESRB is not doing a good job in the way it rates video games. Our little brothers and sisters fit into the range of the people whom E-rated games are meant for. Some of the E-rated games we play are definitely not suitable for young kids.

We don't want our younger siblings playing those games!

The National Institute on Media and the Family's annual report card shows that video games were being rated wrong (or too low). It evaluated ESRB's ratings system and found inaccurate ratings—certain games allow young kids to see things that are unsuitable for their age. We agree with these findings and think that many of the ratings are inappropriate.

In addition to inappropriate ratings, video games rated Teen, Mature, and Adult Only are being sold to young kids. Even at our school, kids are buying unsuitable video games. Forty-six percent of fourth graders at Concord Road Elementary School in Ardsley, N.Y., admitted to buying a video game rated Teen, Mature, or Adult Only. We think this is outrageous. The ratings are supposed to prevent kids from buying inappropriate games, but apparently this system is not working.

The ESRB's ratings system needs to include detailed descriptions of violent or mature content, as well as whether players are required to injure characters in order to achieve the goals of the game. Parents and children have to educate themselves about the ESRB rating system and the specific game they want to purchase.

We also think that retailers should be required by law to sell only age-appropriate video games to minors (those under 18). Stores who don't comply with these laws should be fined or lose their license to sell video games.

Maybe these things will get better in the future, but right now ESRB ratings are flawed, parents and kids are misinformed, and some stores are selling inappropriate video games to kids. So we say—why take a chance in playing video games at all?

Should Kids Play Video Games?

Cast Your Vote

You have read our arguments for playing video games.

ALI BOHRER   MADISON DINASO   LAWRENCE SLOANE   ALEC EISENBERG

RACHEL WEINSTEIN   ALEX GELB   ISAMU KUBO   TAKUYA HATTA

You have read our arguments against playing video games.

JOSH BERLOWITZ   MAIKA IKEBE   JULIE KIM   TYLER FODIMAN   EMILY GREENWALD

TORI MORANO   ETHAN ADER   LUCAS CAHN-EVANS   DANIEL WEBER   JESSICA TILLES   RYAN ROSENBERG

Now add up your points and cast your vote.
Are you FOR or AGAINST kids playing video games?

Our Authors at Work

How We Wrote Our Persuasive Book

For six weeks, we worked with our teacher, Mrs. Peterson. We began by studying persuasive texts and practicing how to debate various issues. As a class, we created a list of possible topics to write about. When we started to analyze video games, we knew we had a lot to say on the topic. We decided to write a persuasive book that looked at all the positive and negative arguments about playing video games. This is how we came to write *Should Kids Play Video Games?*

We thought it would be pretty easy, but it was challenging at times. We all had opinions about playing video games, but we knew they weren't enough. We needed to do a lot of research to learn more about video games. It was amazing how much our writing grew from beginning to end. Here are the steps we took to write our persuasive text.

1. We listed all the issues that had to do with playing video games and wrote about them in our Writer's Notebooks.

2. We selected the issues that we thought were most important. We talked about these issues and started to form our opinions. We listed all of our arguments, for and against playing video games. Each of us chose the argument he or she felt most strongly about.

3. We took our key arguments and formulated them into writing.

4. We started researching our arguments. We spent a lot of time searching the Internet. We also read newspaper and magazine articles. Some of us did surveys of students at our school.

5. Our teacher taught us many ways to improve our writing. We practiced writing strong introductions, powerful conclusions, and great paragraphs. We learned how to use interesting vocabulary, facts to support our opinions, and persuasive language.

6. After doing lots of reading, note taking, and debating the issues, we drafted our pieces.

7. Next, we worked together with our peers to revise and edit our writing.

8. Finally, we typed our first draft and sent it to the editor.

9. We received our first drafts from the editor, and we all had to make changes to our work.

10. We began revising our drafts. We were studying how to make our pieces much better.

11. When we finished fixing up our drafts, we typed them and sent them to the editor for the last time.

12. Finally, we finished our pieces. We invited our parents to school and celebrated our writing. We all learned so much about video games and writing persuasive texts.

Glossary

addiction	attachment to something; when you can't stop doing something
adequate	enough, satisfactory
aggressive	quick to attack or start a fight
analyze	to study something to find out what it is or if it will work
appropriate	suitable
budget	a certain amount of money
content	what something is made up of
debate	to argue for or against something
desensitize	to get used to bad things (such as violence) and think they're not bad anymore
develop	to create
entertainment	something fun
inaccurate	not correct

industry	a job, work, or business that provides certain goods
interacting	doing something together
monitor	to check for a specific reason
outrageous	going beyond what is normal or right
pulse rate	how fast your heart is beating
purchase	to buy something
realistic	true to life
reduce	to make smaller
routines	regular ways of doing things
sensor	equipment that responds to a stimulus
siblings	brothers and/or sisters
simulate	to imitate
specifically	for one purpose
strategy	a careful plan
stress	physical or mental tension
viewing	watching or seeing something
violence	very strong physical force

Bibliography

Carolipio, Redmond. "Industry Put on Defensive." Inland Valley Daily Bulletin. 23 March 2005. http://www.dailybulletin.com/Stories/0,1413,203%257E21481%257E2777250,00.html.

"Children Spend More Time Playing Video Games Than Watching TV." 2 April 2004. Michigan State University. 17 March 2005. <http://www.newsroom.msu.edu/site/indexer/1943/content.htm>.

"Computer and Video Game Addiction." 15 Oct. 2002. National Institute on Media and the Family. 22 Feb. 2005. <http://www.mediafamily.org/facts/facts_gameaddiction.shtml>.

"ESRB Game Ratings: Game Rating & Descriptor Guide." Entertainment Software Rating Board. http://www.esrb.org/esrbratings_guide.asp. 4 April 2005.

Funk, J.B. (1993). "Reevaluating the Impact of Video Games." *Clinical Pediatrics*, 32 (2 Feb.): 86–90. PS 521 243.

Funk, J. B., J. Hagan, and J. Schimming. (1999). "Children and Electronic Games: A Comparison of Parents' and Children's Perceptions of Children's Habits and Preferences in a United States Sample." *Psychological Reports*, 85, 883–888.

"Media Violence Facts and Statistics." National Youth Violence Prevention Resource Center. 23 Feb. 2005. <http://www.safeyouth.org/scripts/faq/mediaviolstats.asp>.

Peck, Peggy. 2 Dec. 2002. "Violent Video Games Shown to Affect Brain Cells." 23 Feb. 2005. <http://www.rense.com/general32/brainc.htm>.

"Rating Video Games: A Cautionary Tale From a Harvard Study." *The Lion and Lamb Project*. 28 Feb. 2005. http://www.lionlamb.org/vid_games_cautionary_tale.htm.

"A Real Attention Getter." *Scientific and Technical Information (STI)*. 16 March 2005. <http://www.sti.nasa.gov/tto/spinoff2003/hm_2.html>.

"Some Video Games Used as Physical Therapy, Phobia Treatment." *The Orange County Register*. 25 Feb. 2005. <http://radio.ksl.com/index.php?nid+104&sid=152778>.

Song, Elisa Hae-Jung and Jane E. Anderson. "How Violent Games May Violate Children's Health." *Contemporary Pediatrics*. May 2001. 23 Feb. 2005. http://lists.essential.org/pipermail/commercial-alert/2001/000079.html.

"Video Violence Can Have Profound Negative Impact." 23 Feb. 2005. <http://www.fradical.com/video_violence_can_have_profound.htm>.

"Violent Video Game Pulled From Shelves." 29 July 2004. *MSNBC*. 23 Feb. 2005. <http://www.msnbc.com/id/5550010>.

Wald, Mark. "Columbine Families Sue Computer Game Makers." BBC News Online. 1 May 2001. <http://news.bbc.co.uk/2/hi/science/nature/1295920.stm>. 4 April 2005.

Walsh, David, Douglas Gentile, Jeremy Gieske, Monica Walsh, and Emily Chasco. "Mediawise Video Game Report Card." 23 Nov. 2004. National Institute on Media and the Family. http://www.mediafamily.org.

Index